networking*works!*

introduction

Thank you for joining us on this exciting journey. Your presence here is an indication that you recognize the power of a good referral based networking plan and are committed to networking as the foundation of building your business.

We will teach you how to build your networking plan and leverage key relationships to meet your professional goals.

Networking definition: the process of building relationships for mutual gain. You can build relationships for mutual ***personal*** gain – such as finding a spouse. You can build relationships for mutual ***family*** gain – such as establishing a carpool for your kids' soccer practice. Or, you can build relationships for mutual ***professional*** gain – such as increasing your access to qualified prospects and expanding your reach of services offered.

The **networking***works!* program is designed to teach you everything you need to know to access a higher level of relationships and more qualified referrals.

Effective networking will increase your performance and help you maximize sustainable revenue and profits. This will be through the strategic application of proven behaviors. The **networking***works!* program is about taking the work out of networking and netting better business results.

evaluation

What are your biggest networking challenges?

1. ______________________________
2. ______________________________
3. ______________________________
4. ______________________________

How much is networking worth to your business this year?

Impact is contingent on:

~ The number of people you meet.

~ The number of referrals per person each year.

~ Your average dollar sale.

~ The number of years you keep the relationship strong.

These are not additive, they are multiplicative. Is this potential compelling to you? What would happen if you played around with each of these factors over time? What is your long term potential?

BIGGEST NETWORKING CHALLENGES (circle all that apply)

1. Getting started.
2. Starting a conversation with someone you don't know.
3. Transitioning a friend to become a business partner.
4. Identifying the right group to join to get business contacts.
5. Setting goals.
6. Staying motivated.
7. Differentiating myself from the competition.
8. Following up with people.
9. Finding effective tools I can use.
10. Building relationships quickly.

past experiences

positive examples - what went well? why?

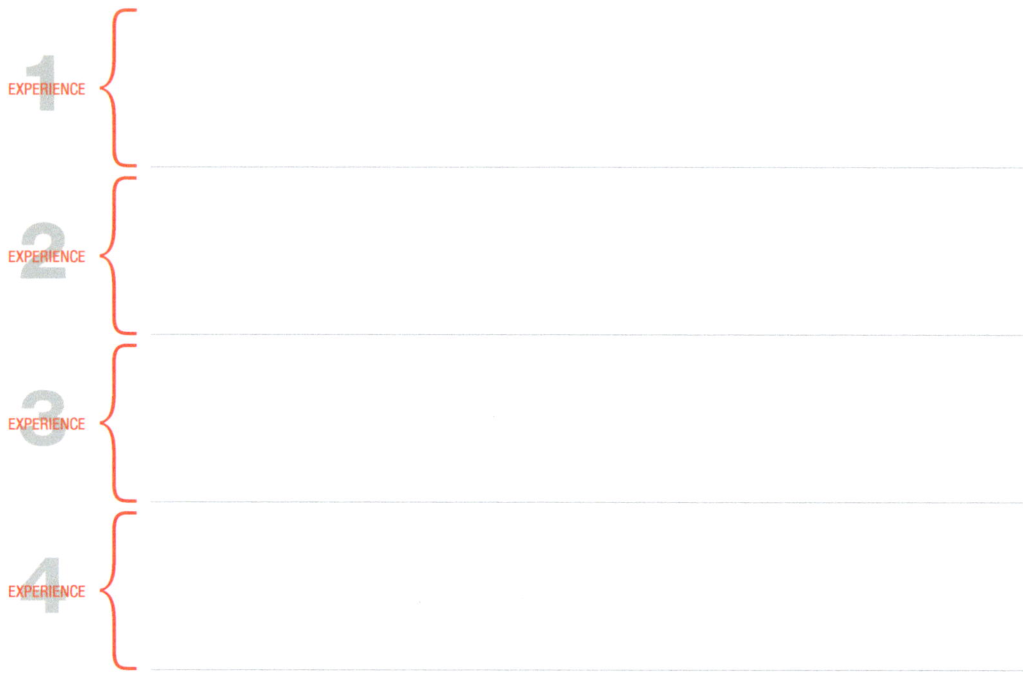

negative examples - what went poorly? why?

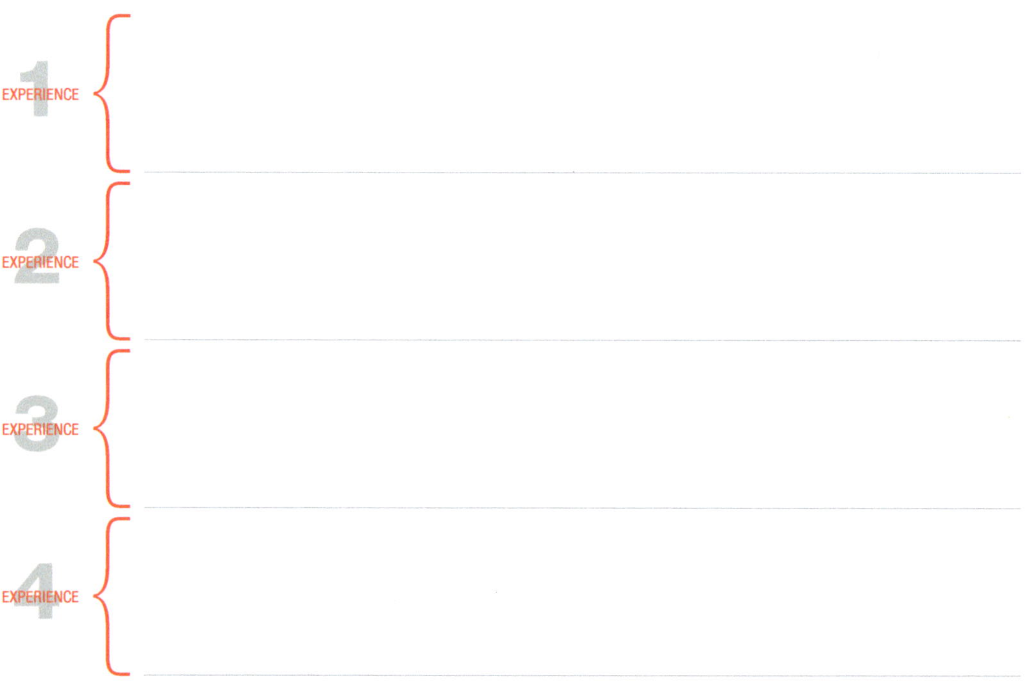

the problem –

Most positive networking experiences can be attributed to success in the following areas:

~ Clearly defined goals and strategies to achieve the goals.

~ Proper mind set and attitude for success.

~ Preparation and practice implementing the key strategies.

~ Execution of the implementation plan.

Most negative networking experience challenges can be attributed to a failure in following areas:

~ No system, strategy or goals for networking.

~ Limiting ourselves through feelings of stress and fear.

~ Under preparing for important connections.

the solution –

networking*works!* program

...is a 13-step system for networking.

Your Customized Networking Implementation Plan details your strategy for program implementation.

Practice the system to reduce stress, increase confidence, and secure the proper mind-set and attitude.

Put the plan into action.

13 programsteps

Setting Smart Goals:

Preparing for the Program

	LAST 12 MONTHS	NEXT 12 MONTHS
12 month trailing revenue		
$ Revenue from referrals		
% Revenue from referrals		

List the people you already work with who bring you business
(directly or indirectly); or who support your business success:

Prepare Your Foundation

FOUNDATIONAL ELEMENTS

Rate yourself on these 4 foundational elements (be honest): **1** (low) **10** (high)

C

Commitment to the process:

Are you willing to step outside of your comfort zone to build a strong network?

Rating: ________

A

Attitude:

Do you have a positive attitude or do you shrink away from the planning, practice and implementation?

Rating: ________

P

Passion for your networking need:

Are you passionate about your product or service?

Rating: ________

R

Responsibility:

Do you take responsibility for your behaviors and actions?

Rating: ________

my lowest rated foundational element is:

WHY?

____

Actions to Maintain Your Foundation

Commitment Actions:

~ Remind yourself of the goal and the outcome you desire.

~ Select a buddy to partner with to motivate you to stay committed.

Attitude Actions:

~ Engage in smile therapy.

~ Dress for success.

~ Fake it 'til you make it!

Passion Actions:

~ Love the one you're with.

~ Begin the job search process.

~ Reduce or eliminate the negatives in your current job.

Responsibility Actions:

~ Prescribe to a form of accountability tracking.

~ Journal.

Weekly actions I will take to maintain my foundational elements?

(write which one will be your focus)

What will you do? ______________________________

____

How? ______________________________

____

Deadline? ______________________________

Some of the other things you can do to be prepared:

Carry professional business cards – lots of them. Consider carrying a card case. Card cases are inexpensive and look professional. Keep some in your car, your briefcase, your wallet.

Consider carrying a card file of your favorite product/service providers. Carry cards for all of the business people you would gladly refer. When someone has a need, you can make the referral on the spot.

Give two of your cards whenever you give yours away ….. one for them, one to give away to a colleague or friend who needs your services/product. You may even consider coding the back of the card so when you receive an enquiry, you can trace where it came from.

Remember: When someone gives you their business card, take a moment to look at the card. Don't just stuff it in your pocket or handbag. Write something on it about the person, before you drop it in your bag. Ask who a good referral is for them. Transfer this data into your client management system so you can access it again.

Dress professionally. While we all know we should not judge a book by it's cover, the first impression is made within 3-10 seconds. And it's harder to change a first impression than to create one. Be clear on what impression you want to make, and then maximize your first impression.

Make sure you have a firm handshake. Approach people with confidence. Extend your right hand for a shake. Make eye contact and smile. If you are in a bad mood, use smile therapy. It works! Pick the right time to approach people you don't know. Or better yet, get an introduction.

Define Your Target Market

Let's begin by getting very clear on your target market. Who are your targets? What do they look like, act like, want, need, own, wear, etc.? Define your target market.

Think about your ideal customer/business.

List the characteristics of your ideal customer/business in detail. Consider things like demographics, needs, niches: gender, age/age of business, income level, sales/revenue, location, number of employees, area of town/market. Look at specific problems they need to solve. Identify the unique niches that differentiate your business.

List the characteristics of your ideal customer/business in detail.

If you're stuck, list the things you love about your favorite customers:

Now list the things you dislike about your least favorite customers, and convert these dislikes into a positive "ideal" characteristic:

Now, given that target market (ideal customer), who do you want to know? Be specific: List industries, companies, categories of people, and names. Use resources such as the Business Journal Book of Lists, Chamber of Commerce databases, and library resources.

Once you know who you want to know, the next step is to determine…

Who knows who you want to know?

This is your **Target Market** and **Target Market Net**

My Target Market	Who knows them? Who might know them? What groups would them belong to?	How will I meet them?

Now you have the data and descriptors you need to network more strategically. Ask friends, family members, business colleagues: "Who do you know who…?" Most people want to help others, so if you are clear on who you want to know, and you discover who knows them, build that relationship until you can be comfortable asking for an introduction. People will often make an introduction for you if they know you, like you, and trust you.

Emotionally Engage Your Network

In order to build a strong network of referrals, you must also be able to engage your network in what you do. In this chapter we are going to cover the first important component of that, your Unique Selling Proposition, the tag line of your uniqueness. Later, we will design your 10 second, 30 second and 60 second commercial so you can engage others in conversation.

Your Unique Selling Proposition (USP):

~ It is 1-2 sentences.

~ It is clearly defined, so that anyone can understand it.

~ It's believable.

It is composed of 1-2 unique emotionally compelling reasons to do business with your company, or 1-2 problems your company uniquely solves. Your USP is the emotional compelling reason to do business with your company.

Your USP should answer the following questions:

~ What benefit is unique to your offering? What niche do you fill? Why?

~ Who is the target market for whom this benefit is of compelling interest? Why?

~ What pain or pleasure does your product/service eliminate or offer?

~ How will your product help them solve that pain/problem?

~ What is your competition claiming? How are you different?

Your USP should describe the benefit your target market gets from your product or service. Differentiate this from a feature. A feature is a 'nice to have' about the product or service. A benefit is a solution to a problem or need your target market has. In step 2, you defined your target market. You know who they are and what they are about. This will help you define what they would consider a benefit!

How are you different from your competition? Remember, competitors may be direct – they do exactly what you do. Or they may be indirect – they compete for the same dollars you compete for. Instead of challenging your competitor directly on their uniqueness, find a different angle where you can offer your target market a different benefit/solution.

Developing Your USP

List all the reasons someone would do business with you.

Which ones trigger an emotional response from your clients? Circle them.
Why do they trigger an emotional response?

List the most significant problems you uniquely solve:

Which ones are most important to your best clients? Circle them.
Which ones are hardest for your competition to imitate?

now, let's do the same for your competitors:

List the reasons someone would do business with your competitors:

Which trigger an emotional response or are most compelling?

List all the problems they uniquely solve.

Based on this comparison to your competition, and the understanding of your unique compelling emotional reasons, **What is your unique competitive advantage?**

Combine these concepts into a 1-2 line memorable statement that speaks to the unique, meaningful qualities about your business or brand. Make sure it's a message that speaks to the need your prospective customer has. Also, make sure it does not say anything negative about your competition. Now you have a USP. Practice speaking and refining it until it feels natural and captures your uniqueness.

Determine Your Prospects

If your network or prospects don't emotionally engage with what you do or who you are, they won't be a strong referral source or prospect for you.

The 60-second elevator speech provides a brief overview of your business, and it is designed to entice a prospect to want to learn more.

However, most people will not listen to anyone talk for 60 seconds about what they do. This may be especially true in a social or business situation. You may have reason to speak for 60 seconds during a networking referrals or lead group, or at a business training function during introductions; so it is important to be prepared. Those situations will look like information sharing, not networking conversations.

During networking conversations (and most other times), the average attention span is less than 15 seconds, so you must have a teaser talk ready that will briefly describe enough of what you do so that you and the recipient can both assess whether there is reason to talk further.

A good elevator speech will help you quality your clients. You will know if they are interested in what you do; or, if there is no immediate interest. That way you don't waste your time in business conversation with them if they are not interested.

Develop Your 10-second Teaser

This is a teaser, so it should be short and enticing.

who do you serve?

{ ______________________________

what problems do you solve?

{ ______________________________

Develop Your 60-second Elevator Speech

A powerful elevator speech contains the following:

Grab their attention by stating:

~ Who are you?

~ What do you do?

~ What is unique about your business/company?

~ What are the key benefits of your products or services? Describe it through a story, example, anecdote.

~ What problems do you solve for your customers/clients that they have told you are important to them? Describe the problems you have solved and the impact the solution had on the client's business.

~ What is your memory hook?

Pull data from your USP and your business and marketing plan. Be specific.

avoid...

~ Industry language that most people won't understand.

~ Apologies or excuses for anything you do or say.

~ Giving too many details about your company, or about what you do. Keep your description big picture.

~ Bragging about your service or value. Instead, give examples about it.

Writing a Powerful 60-second Elevator Speech

30 - 60 second commercial sample:

My name is ______________________________, with ___________________________.

Our target market is: ____. Our typical client: ____________________________________ (insert problems you solve). They choose to work with us because: ____ (insert your emotionally compelling USP.) A good referral for me is: ___________________________ __________________ (name/companies or describe kinds of industries/businesses that meet the criteria above).

Identify 5-10 Key Relationships

that can Revolutionize Your Business

Remember, the intent of networking is to BUILD RELATIONSHIPS. Networking is not selling. Networking is building meaningful relationships. People do business with those they KNOW, LIKE and TRUST. So, you are building relationships to build your business. Your prospects must know you, like you, and trust you in order to become clients.

Building your six degrees of Kevin Bacon 'Relationship Net' recognizes that we live in a small world, and we can connect to anyone we want to know through fewer than six people. The key is to figure out who we want to know and build our net to encompass them, or those who know them.

The implications of this are significant. It means that your ideal prospects are only six introductions (max!) away from you. If your market is local or in the state of North Carolina, for example, you may need even fewer connections.

A study called the Small World Experiment sought to define how many people each of us know, on average, and map how many connections we need to reach anyone in the world. This and other studies on social networks indicated that the average person knows 250 people, and anyone in the world can be reached through just 3-6 connections.

Your 6º of Kevin Bacon 'Relationship Net'

Let's just play around with that idea a little bit.

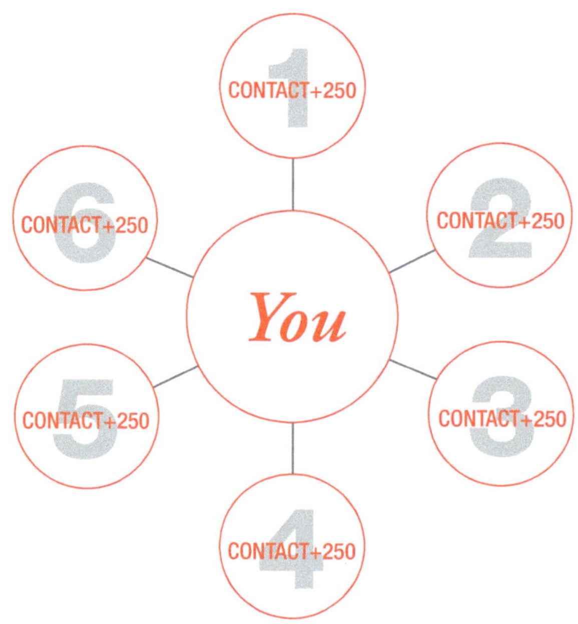

You should be able to connect to one of your 250 people, who knows one of their 250 people who knows… who knows your ideal prospect.

isn't that powerful?

Even if you don't totally buy into this theory, you can certainly agree that there are people you know who know people you want to know. You can also probably agree that the scope of the community you are trying to reach is much smaller than the scope of the small world experiment.

We're going to analyze additional connections you can leverage as referral sources over the next few pages.

Expand Your Net:

Benefit Net

What industries/companies get business when you get business?

THEY ARE YOUR BENEFIT NET:

Company	Name	Strategy to Meet	Organizations They May Belong To

examples:

~ **Banker:** CPA, investment advisor/financial planner, tax attorney, commercial insurance, management consultant, payroll services, etc.

~ **High-end furniture manufacturer:** retail accessories, carpet, home improvements, reupholster, moving company, clothier, etc.

~ **Wedding planner:** chauffeur, dress/tuxedo shop, florist, bridal store, videographer, photographer, travel agent, etc.

~ **Realtor:** mortgage broker, inspector, attorney, home furnishings, appraiser, builder/re-modeler, etc.

Expand Your Net Again:
Jealousy Net

Who does business with people you want to do business with?

Whose client list are you jealous of?

Company	Name	Strategy to Meet	Organizations They May Belong To

examples:

~ **Banker:** business attorney, CPA, financial planner, etc.

~ **High-end furniture manufacturer:** high-end home builder, high-end car dealership, expensive travel destinations, etc.

~ **Wedding planner:** newspaper engagement announcement editor, Belk/Dillard shopping, etc.

Expand Your Net Again:

'They Like Me' Net

These are the people who you have given business to for whatever reason. Who have you referred business to in the past six months?

Company	Name	Strategy to Meet	Organizations They May Belong To

Expand Your Net Again:

'I Like Them' Net

These are the people you have received business from in the past six months – for whatever reason?

Company	Name	Strategy to Meet	Organizations They May Belong To

Expand Your Net Again:

Alliance Net

What kind of win-win alliances could you form to maximize an aspect of your business? Who could you co-market or co-sell with? Who could you offer alliance services with? How could you expand your client base through this approach? Think about customers, suppliers, mentors, and competitors. Look for abundance, not scarcity.

Company	Name	Strategy to Meet	Organizations They May Belong To

Expand Your Net Again:

Client Net

Who have you worked with already who loves what you do for them? Satisfied, thrilled customers are the best source for ongoing referrals and connections.

Company	Name	Strategy to Meet	Organizations They May Belong To

Building Your Referral Net

From the expanded net resources in the previous sections, list the most significant relationships that will be most likely to bring business benefit and profit for your business.

The most significant networking/referral relationships:

The secondary networking relationships that either need further development or will take more time for the same profitability and visibility, but still offer great win-win reward potential:

You may want to draw these relationships as a mind map to look for other synergies, interrelationships and connections as you develop them over time. It can also be useful to map how you've connected to key people over your years in business. This map can help you glean who are your key connector sources and help you identify where have you seen the most financial reward. See Mind Map below.

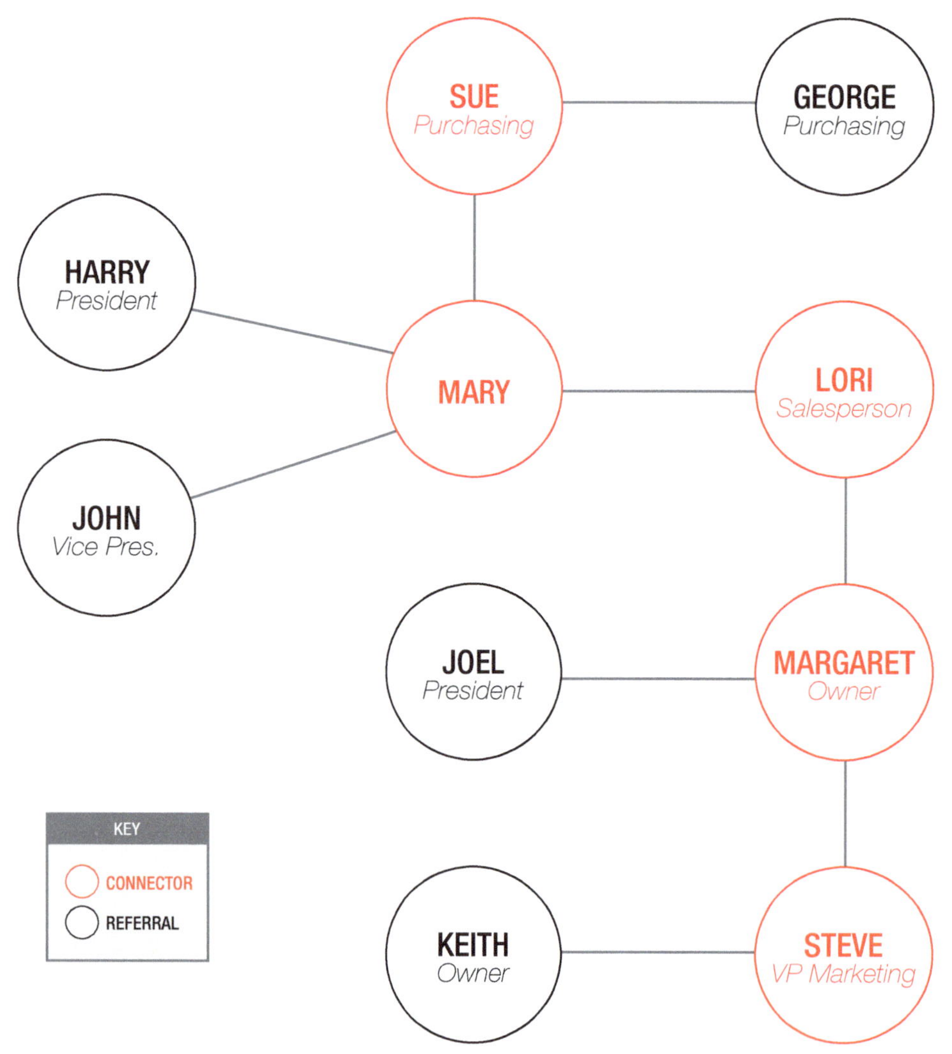

Join Strategic Organizations

Get Involved

We know that the best way to meet new people and build strong relationships is to join an organization that interests you. The best way to form strong relationships is to be an active part of that same organization.

Think back to how you met your closest friends or your spouse. Chances are high that you met them through some formal or informal organization you participated in. It could be a hiking club, a church group, a volunteer organization, or, maybe it was through your children's activities. The more you engaged in the organization(s), the broader and deeper you built the relationships.

As you prepare your networking plan, it is important to be very strategic and deliberate in your choice of what organization to join. Joining an organization that includes the key people in your prospecting and referral nets is a top priority. How do you decide which to join?

What organization(s) interest you?

If you are not interested in the organization, it is likely you will not make the commitment to it.

What organization(s) showed up multiple times in your key relationship nets?

What other organization(s) could you consider? (See list on next page.)

What organization(s) does your jealousy net participate in?

Where do those who compete with or complement your services/ products join? Your alliance net may join these.

What organization(s) do your current customers participate in?

What organization(s) does your 'They Like Me' net participate in?

Types of Organizations

Consider the following types of organizations as ticklers to get you started:

Civic/Service

Rotary

Kiwanis

Lions Club

Leadership/Prof.Dev.

Jaycees

Speakers Bureau

Toastmasters

Chamber Leadership Dev.

Vistage

Industry Specific

ASTD

Amer. Management Assoc.

Amer. Marketing Assoc.

Inter. Coach Federation

Builder Association

Realtors Association

Church/Temple

Faith Formation

Pre-Cana

Interfaith Hospitality

Arts

Community Theater

United Arts Council

Social

Singles Clubs

Dance Groups

Business

Chamber

Vistage

Exec. Roundtable

Online

LinkedIn

Facebook

Twitter

Community

Country Clubs

Non-profits

Sports (play, coach)

Golf League

Basketball League

Soccer League

Youth Sports

Professional Sports

Networking

Leads Groups

BNI

Network USA

Women's Groups

ABWA

eWomen Network

NAWBO

Hobbies

Other

Where can you find out about the organizations that will serve you best?

~ Internet search for industry-specific, nationwide

~ Chamber of Commerce

~ Newspapers: local, business

~ Talk to people!

It's important to prioritize the organizations you will join so you don't spread yourself too thin. We recommend selecting a mix of organizations that will give you different exposure points to your prospect and referral nets, and engage you in ways that are personally and professionally rewarding.

Considerations:

How often the organizations meet.

Organizations that meet frequently may enable faster relationship building and a larger time commitment.

The number of members in the organization.

Larger organizations may have more prospects and it may be more difficult to build fast relationships.

The structure of the organization and the leadership.

Will you enjoy being a part of it? Is the leadership organized, focused? Do you prefer flexibility and spontaneity?

The opportunity to get involved.

Is there opportunity to get involved in a way that plays to your strengths and interests?

The cost.

Is it in your budget? Is it worth the investment of time, money and other resources to you?

Ask members about their experience with the organization. Visit meetings to form an impression.

Organizations I am active in	Benefit	Decision

Organizations to visit this quarter	Benefit	Implications

Once you join the organization, look for ways to get involved. It's this active participation that enables you to build stronger relationships and showcase who you are and what you do. Consider holding an office, joining the Board of Directors, leading a committee or project, or other visible positions. It will require additional time, but the relationships you form will be worth the exchange – if you choose your organizations and leadership positions wisely.

Remember that building relationships is a process that takes time. Be willing to commit a ***minimum*** of six months – more likely a year – to any organization you join before expecting direct results from your relationship-building work. That is why it is important to choose wisely.

Building Your Personal Board of Directors

Everything we do requires support from other people. Who do you have in place to consciously and pro-actively support you? You can leave that support to chance. You can leave that support to you manager or suppliers, friends or colleagues; or, you can consciously, proactively build that support into your professional life. We recommend strategically building in the support that will serve you best. We call that support your *Board of Directors*.

Your *Board of Directors* is a group of people who are willing to help you achieve your goals. They provide resources, time and energy in areas where you have professional needs or wants. They may be mentors who want to share their wisdom and experience with you in exchange for the opportunity to revel in your successes. They may be colleagues or customers who can give you referrals and benefit from your business growth. They may be friends or family who always seem to be able to help you focus, regroup or calm down and put things into perspective.

The only criteria for a *Board of Directors* member is that they want you to be successful and they are willing to share their time, energy, resources and referrals with you to help you do that.

In some cases, you may provide something tangible back to them, such as referrals or a barter of services. In some cases, you may provide them with a very different return on their investment. For instance, you may become a trusted colleague to confer with on their business. Or, you may keep them pumped up about their career. Or, you may support them in other ways. Look for people who have the skills, experience, and wisdom you need, and offer them the opportunity to join your *Board of Directors*. Then discover what you can offer them in return for their support.

Who will you ask to join your personal *Board of Directors*?

STEP 1: Review your business goals and strategies for the year.

Your goals and strategies will drive the resources that will be the best support for you.

My key goals and strategies for this year are:

STEP 2: Identify key resources who you believe can best help fill those needs. Put a list together of possible people you could tap into for support.

FOR EACH YOU NEED TO CONSIDER:

~ Experts in your field who have retired or moved to a different industry:

~ Competitors who are much bigger or smaller than you, or are focusing in a different target market or a different niche:

~ People who coach and/or train people in your industry:

~ People who have mentored you:

~ People you have given referrals to or supported in any way:

~ People you have gone to training, classes, programs, seminars, or school with:

~ Family, friends, co-workers, boss, neighbors (current and past):

~ People you have met through clubs, groups, organizations, such as church, community involvement, civic, etc:

~ People who you see as very successful (just a thought):

Who do you know, like, and trust to help you from this comprehensive list?

STEP 3: Enrolling them.

Most people love to help others. Define your needs and how you think your Personal Board of Directors could help you meet them. Ask them if they would be willing to participate. Be clear on your expectations and their commitment up front, and be sure to ask about their needs in return. The best success team members have a clearly defined win-win situation. The worst thing that can happen is that they say "no," or "not now."

You may consider doing an informal "give/get" process with each Personal Board of Directors participant:

Define your needs/requests of them: (your "gets" / their "gives")	Define your needs/requests of you in return: (your "gives" / their "gets")

Negotiate with them to set up the best win-win partnership and agree to revisit the "gives/gets" periodically.

STEP 4: Getting started.

The ideal personal Board of Directors size is 4-8 people. Why? Each person will require an ongoing commitment of time and energy from you to build and maintain a strong relationship. Most people don't have the time to maintain close relationships with more than about 4-8 people. If you do, expand your personal Board of Directors.

A. Organizing your Personal Board of Directors

Will you meet together as a group? Or, will you meet with each member one-on-one? If you meet as a group, be conscious of how you are using the time together to ensure you are making good use of all of your Personal Board of Directors members' time. Group meetings can offer incredible synergy and a flow of ideas. Consider using them as problem solving meetings and taping the session for future review. (Be sure to ask permission from the team members before taping). Meeting one-on-one can provide focus and penetration on a particular challenge, and can offer you undivided time with your resource.

Group meeting? ___________ 1:1 Meeting? _____________

B. Determining meeting frequency

Will you meet monthly? Quarterly? As needed?

Meeting frequency: __________________

C. Developing your agenda

Will it be a problem solving session, a feedback session for you, or a brainstorming session? How will you plan the time to get the most out of it? The clearer you are on the objective and flow of the meeting process, the more benefit you and your Personal Board of Directors members will get from the session. If you have a very important meeting, consider hiring a professional facilitator to help keep your agenda on track and take chart pad notes.

D. Follow up

What follow up do you need from your Board of Directors members? Document it, and hold them accountable to deliver it. What follow up do they need from you? Document that and be accountable. Do what you say you will do. It reinforces your credibility and their desire to support you.

List your personal *Board of Directors* notes here:

Your personal *Board of Directors* will develop and mature over time. Some members may transition out and new members may join in. The relationships you establish through this process will breed a strong commitment to help you become successful, and isn't that what this process is all about?

Be Interested & Interesting

Now that you have your net identified, it's very important that you know how to build meaningful relationships. How you create the ongoing network of people who know you, like you and trust you. The key is to be interested and interesting.

Remember as John Maxwell says, "People don't care how much you know until they know how much you care."

Engage people in conversation about their favorite topic: them! Use their name in conversation. People love to hear their own name used. Shake their hand firmly when you first meet them. A firm handshake communicates confidence.

Ask them targeted questions about themselves, and their work. Find out their professional and personal interests, what they do outside of work, their weekend plans....Be authentic, care about what is important to them.

Take notes on the back of their business card. Write it all down. If you don't have their business card, ask for it! If they are reluctant to give it to you, offer to send them some information on a topic of interest to them; and then do it!

When you take notes on their business card it send the message that what they are saying is important to you. When you go back through your cards the next day, it also helps you remember what they said and what you committed to do.

You will not be successful telling them how great your product or service is until you know enough about them to know if they care. And you don't want to waste time telling them about your great product or service if they are not a good prospect for you. Pre-qualify them by caring enough to find out.

Share with them what you do. Be brief and succinct. Focus on the problems you solve. Pull in examples that fit what you have just learned about them.

If you believe there is mutual interest, set up a time to reconnect to continue the conversation. Then move on…to your next networking prospect.

"Be interested and interesting." This means speaking well of others. Always! Resist the temptation to engage in negative conversation about anyone else. It may feel like a good opportunity to bond with another person, but the risks are significant that it will come back to haunt you, and will mar future relationships. You may get a reputation you don't want, and it's harder to shake a bad reputation than to build one from scratch.

Speak well of your competitors, your clients, and your network. Rave, if you can. Be a walking testimonial for other people's services. It will reflect well on you, too.

Use the following questions to help you engage people in conversation.

Questions for new and developing relationships:

1. How long have you been in this business/industry?
2. How did you get into this line of work?
3. What do you enjoy most about your work?
4. What do you do to promote/sell your business?
5. What is your ideal client? How would I recognize them?
6. What are the most significant benefits your clients receive from working with you?
7. What is new and exciting in your business/industry?
8. What activities are most profitable or productive for you?
9. How has your industry changed over the past 10 years?
10. What do you do for fun?

Learn More
About Your Network

Are they big picture or detail oriented?

Are they introverts or extroverts?

Are they analytical or people oriented?

Are they task oriented or spontaneous?

Are they visual, auditory, kinesthetic?

What are some of their favorite expressions?

Tailoring Your Questions

When you are in a networking situation, it's helpful to have a list of questions that can quickly help you in conversation and also evaluate if someone is a good prospect for your business. Your 60 second commercial will introduce that. This tailored question list will take it a step further. Remember, people most enjoy talking about themselves, so building a list of questions about them will facilitate a more productive and interesting conversation.

Building your question list:

What might you be interested in knowing about someone to determine if they might ever be a prospect for you? Consider questions that give you information to help you evaluate if they fit your target market description first. Then go a level deeper, towards your pre-qualification criteria. Be careful not to ask questions that get too personal for a networking environment.

Let's look at a few examples of questions built using this process:

Realtor/Moving company/Mortgage broker might ask questions like:

~ What part of town do you live in?
~ How long have you lived there?
~ What do you like about your neighborhood?
~ Where did you move from?

A re-modeler might ask:

~ Where do you live?
~ How long have you lived there?
~ What do you like most about your house?
~ What would you change if you could wave a magic wand?

IT Consultant/technology/web design company might ask questions like:

~ What kind of business are you in?

~ What kinds of technology does your company use every day? (Blackberry, iPhone, web, etc…?)

~ Is your company on the leading edge of technology or are you late adopters?

~ How do you leverage technology to be more effective?

Attorney/CPA might ask questions like:

~ What's the best business advice you ever received?

~ Who did you receive it from?

~ What are the biggest challenges you face in your line or work? Why?

~ How does the current economy help or hurt your business?

The answers will likely reveal information that will help you establish a relationship and also pre-qualify them in or out of your prospect pool. Through the conversation, you may find other ways to refer them to people in your different 'nets'.

You will likely continue to refine your questions over time.

Write your first cut of questions here:

Deliver Incredible Value
to Your Network

It's a philosophy: Help others mercilessly, with expectation of payback. Listen to people. Hear what they are saying. Look for connections you can make for them, and make them. Ask people who they want to know. Ask them what a good referral is for them. Take notes.

Connect people who you know need to be connected. Become a resource database- A Networking King or Queen. People will always think of you first when they have a need.

Ask yourself every morning: "How can I help someone in their business today?" Set about making that happen. Track what you do for others. Keep notes on the number of referrals you give and how many turn into business. Strive to give two referrals per week or connect two people that need to know each other.

What is a good referral:

1. Prospective buyer has a clearly defined need AND
2. You know a company/person who can fill that need with excellence.

How to make a good referral:

1. Clarify the Prospect's need.
2. Describe the sales person who can fill that need with excellence to confirm the match.
3. Ask the prospect if it would be ok if you had the sales person who can fill the need, give them a call to discuss their need in more detail.

   3A: If the answer is no, the Prospect is either not ready to buy, or does not see the match, or has felt pressure from you. Offer that when he/she is ready to move forward, you would be happy to help them connect to the right sales person.

   3B: If the answer is yes, give the Prospect your sales person's card/contact information, and tell them that YOU will have the sales person call them. This ensures that you properly prepare the sales person to have a productive conversation and it ensures that if the sales person wants the business, they must invest the time/energy to get it.

4. Contact your sales person and give them the Prospect's contact information and share some background information about the prospects needs and how you have positioned the Sales person with them.

5. Ask your sales person to contact the Prospect. Remind the sales person that the Prospect is anxiously awaiting his/her call.

6. Follow up with both the sales person and the Prospect to learn what went well. What can you do differently next time. You may learn things about the sales person's business or the Prospect's needs that will help you in future referrals.

7. Track the results of the referrals you gave.

DO NOT: Just hand the prospect your service provider's card. They may never make the connection. They may lose the card. They may be uncomfortable calling. Connect the service provider to the prospect by making a phone call or personal introduction.

When you connect two people, alert each that the other will be calling. Give a heads up! When you introduce two people to each other, mention something they have in common or say something positive about each that relates to their reason for meeting. People will value and respect that and keep you front-of-mind when they are out and about.

We work with people all day long. We learn about their challenges,needs, strengths, and wants. If we are paying attention, we can find ways to help them through referrals to a great service provider, listening over lunch, sharing good advice, and sharing an experience together.

Give to your customers. Give to your referral network. Give them perks such as logo wear, give them free tickets to an event, invite them to a presentation you are having just for clients.

Ultimately, our success in business comes down to the kind of value and service we provide to our clients and our referral network. If that value is high, they keep coming back for more and are more inclined to refer business. If that value is low, they may tell as many as 20 others about their terrible experience.

Here are some questions to consider as you think about delivering incredible value:

What value do you provide your referral network?

What is their emotional experience of that value?

A. Where is it positive?

B. Where might it be negative?

How do you know?

When was the last time you solicited feedback from your referral network?

What about pay for referrals?

Money or gifts can be great motivators for building lucrative, mutually beneficial business relationships. These tend to work better when built upon a solid foundation of trust, respect and mutual business understanding and support. The most effective way to build these relationships then is to start with the relationship and build to a more formal monetary-based return. Start recognizing the importance of the relationship with small rewards, such as thank you notes, thank you calls, and small tokens of appreciation. Think about it as date – you probably would do small things for a date that you enjoy spending time with, but would not yet give a larger monetary gift. Over time, as the relationship grows and you discover common values, niche opportunities, or a core source of business revenue for you from the relationship, it may be appropriate to build a more serious dating, or maybe even engagement, moving in together or marriage. Time and continued relationship building will tell. Starting with a pay for referral/lead approach can not only have you paying for a lot of leads/referrals that don't deliver revenue, but they also can set up a dynamic where business colleagues under-value your business capability. Sometimes paying a fee for referrals and leads without a more established relationship, can be perceived as cheapening your business. Be aware of the potential before you decide to move forward. You can always offer a financial incentive after you get the business from a lead or referral, if you feel the relationship is strong and supportive of that. Then it becomes a thank you instead of an incentive.

So if you don't use monetary rewards, how can you add even more value? You need to better understand your personal unique value!

What are your greatest strengths? What do you do naturally better than most people? What assets do you have that have excess capacity?

How can you more effectively leverage those to help select people in your referral network?

For example: One asset I have that has excess capacity is that I am a natural connector of people. When I meet someone new, my mind is instantaneously connecting what I am learning about them to all the other resources I have been in contact with over my business career. When I find a connection, I test it with the new person to find out if this connection would be of benefit to them. If so, I make arrangements to do a strong referral, as described earlier in step 8. If not, I simply file their information away into my mental and physical databases. My network now comes to me for introductions because they know I will use my connections to help them and those they know be more successful. It is easy and fun for me to do this, and it adds tremendous value to my referral network.

When we can leverage our strengths, assets with excess capacity, and natural abilities to our referral network's advantage, we build good will and better relationships which will pay dividends to us many times over.

When we help our referral network be more successful, in whatever value added way we do, we all win. They win with more qualified prospects, and we win through building good will and increasing our successful referral out rate.

Design Your Referral System

In this step, we will introduce two approaches to building your ongoing referral system. Both can be used very effectively in any business. The first approach is designing a direct referral system. This sets you up to continue to reap referrals from both your developing network and your client base. Ongoing referrals are the least expensive and highest return on investment. In addition, when you tap into your client base, you are increasing their commitment to you, and they are more likely to know additional prospects who will benefit from your products or services.

How to approach your clients and networks:

1. Share with your clients and networks how much you enjoy doing business with them, or how much you value the relationship you've built.

2. Tell them you have set some goals for yourself and/or your business this year, and ask them if they'd be willing to help you. Conversely, you can tell them you need their help!

3. If they are willing to engage, describe your target market and the problems you want to focus on. Provide enough detail to help them build a clear picture of who they might know who fits that market. Share the names of people or companies you want to do business with. Share industries that fit your market. Tease out ideas by asking "Who do you know who struggles with..." and describe the problems you solve.

4. If nobody comes to mind, they may truly not know anyone or they may not have been honest with you when you asked for their help. Be sensitive to either.

5. You can also pursue other ways they can support you that are less intensive: displaying literature at their place of business, inviting you to a networking event, writing a testimonial for you, etc…

6. If they offer up potential prospects, learn as much as you can about them. Ask them for input on how to approach their referrals.

7. Encourage them to use the process described in Step 8 to make a good referral.

8. Jointly discuss different ways they can introduce you to their referral and agree upon a plan that will be productive and comfortable for both of you. Recognize it's their credibility and reputation that they are using to generate this referral.

9. Go forward with the referral.

10. Follow up afterwards with a handwritten thank you note and any other appropriate gesture of appreciation. Describe the results of the referral meeting or conversation. Consider sending a thank you note to the referral as well, no matter what the outcome of the meeting. It will be an unexpected gesture of appreciation for their time.

If you are using this process with your network, begin the process here:

1. Describe to them in detail the picture of your ideal client. Use your target market description. Build for them a clear picture of who they might know who fits that market. Describe them in terms of characteristics, or offer them names and companies you want to work with. Try the phrase 'Who do you know who… Give them teasers of actions that signal a need for your services or product.

2. Learn as much as you can from them about the people they offer up as potential prospects.

3. Ask them for input on how to approach their referrals.

4. Jointly discuss different ways they can introduce you to that person in a non-threatening way. Be willing to offer the referral a free introductory meeting to discuss and determine if there is even a need for your services. Consider giving them a special rate or adding value in some other way because they are a referral of a client. Also offer your client/network an incentive for each introduction or appointment they set up for you.

5. Proceed with the introductions/appointments.

6. Follow up with your client/network with a handwritten thank you note, the incentive you offered and an update on the results of the meeting. Send a thank you to the referral as well, no matter what the outcome of the meeting.

7. Repeat this process periodically with your clients/network. Also include a reminder on correspondence you send to your network or clients.

When your satisfied clients or networks bring you business, it is good business. It's a win for your clients/networks as well, because they benefit through the appreciation they get from the people who have now become your clients.

The second approach to design your referral system is to set up alliances or other strategic referral-sharing relationships. In some of the earlier steps, you identified the critical relationships for your business. Now, we will design methods to maximize those relationships for your mutual business success. These methods will be win-win's for the key relationships you have been building.

Designing a Strategic Alliance

Another powerful way to design your referral system is to set up alliances or other referral-sharing relationships.

1. Identify the most likely candidates for building a strategic alliance or other partner-type relationship. Look for complementary, non-competitive businesses who use your product or service before or after theirs. You may also find avenues to form alliances with competitors if your product or service fits a different niche than theirs.

List 5 options here:

2. For each of the candidates listed above, discover who their target market is, how they market to those clients today, and what services they offer them.

3. Identify opportunities for:

A. Co-marketing: Ideas include joint sponsorship of an appropriate event, inserting materials in each other's newsletter, use of mail lists.

B. Endorsements of each other's products/services, introductions to each other's client base, or selling each other's products/services.

List your ideas here:

4. Define the win-win benefits for each of you:

A. Project out a benefit and/or compensation package for your alliance partner and for you: Consider: Revenue, profit, cash flow, increase in client base, prestige, better pricing for their clients, more value added, more guarantees.

Benefit to alliance partner:

Benefit to me:

B. Draft out what you are prepared to do:

i. What you will pay for
ii. Guarantees you will offer
iii. Process you will use

What you will do:

C. Draft what you want or need from them: Pilot test a small group, send the mailer, write the endorsement.

Wants/needs from them:

---

5. Engage your proposed alliance partner in discussions to begin to build the win-win process.

Remember, this alliance process is ongoing. It will take time to build the relationship and time to build the systems described in the two sections above, but the investment in building these systems will pay dividends many times over in many ways.

Follow Up.

Consistently. Constantly.

By now you have gathered a lot of wonderful and relevant data about clients, prospects, referral sources and referrals for you. In order to do good follow up, it is important to have a way to keep track of all that data. Taking notes on the back of a business card at an event is a great way to remember the key information for your thank you note the next day, but it is less effective for accessing that information at your fingertips over time.

Build a data base so you can keep track of who you are in touch with and who you need to reconnect with. What you last talked about. What they are looking for. What is important to them.

Follow up is one of the most important steps you can take, so it's important to have access to all the information you gathered through the relationship-building process.

Follow up is simple to do but not always easy. It takes time and it is not always immediately clear the impact it is having on the prospect, client, referral source, referral. It is clear, however, that if you don't follow up, you reduce your opportunity to enroll and/or maintain a client and/or relationship. Most importantly, do what you said you will do. Remember, relationship-building is: know, like, trust... not just know.

FOLLOW UP CAN TAKE MANY FORMS:

Thank you notes:

Send them! Send them to people you meet at networking events, to people you meet for coffee or lunch, to people who do something for you such as connect you to someone else or give you a lead or referral. Send a thank you to someone who simply listened to you when you were stressed out, or offered great advice when you needed it. Remind them of something you learned from them. Share something positive about them or your experience with them. Remind them of a part of the conversation that was significant to you. Connect with them in some special way. Thank them for their time/interest.

Keep a list of who you need to follow up with and take time to do it. It's a professional courtesy and people will be much more likely to remember you.

Think back on the handwritten than you notes you received. Who were they from? What impact did they have on you?

Reconnect phone calls:

Call people in your network periodically …just to say hello. Reconnect on a regular basis. How often is regular? You decide. The key is: How often do you need to connect to stay top of mind when there is a need for your services. For some, it may be monthly. For others, quarterly. And for others yet, maybe weekly!

Think back to the last time someone called you just to reconnect. What did it feel like?

Emails, newsletters, literature, other reminders:

Send your clients, prospects, network an article that they might be interested in. Refer them to a web site with valuable information relevant to their business. It lets them know that they are top of mind for you, and that you are looking for ways to help them be successful.

Think about the newsletters you receive every week. Even if you don't read them, do you remember the sender? Have you ever received unsolicited articles from a colleague about a topic of interest to you?

Commitments:

If you offered or were asked to do something for someone, follow up. Make sure you do what you say you're going to do or proactively renegotiate. The builds trust!

Meetings:

Set up appointments with qualified prospects and key people in your network. Keep abreast of what is going on in their business and keep them abreast of the changes and new directions in your business. Ask for help from them and remember-give, give, give. Connect them formally with the people you think would be most beneficial to them by inviting them both to lunch-with you! It will give you an opportunity to introduce them and help them highlight key connection points.

Referral follow up:

This is a special form of follow up. If you're given a referral or lead, follow up with the prospect immediately! And send a thank you to the person who gave the referral to you! Thank them for their confidence in you. Keep them abreast of the progress you are making and help them understand how to better serve you in the future. If you get a referral that turns into business, consider giving a referral fee or a reward.

After you give a referral, follow up with both the service provider and the client. This gives you critical feedback on the service provider, the client and the relationship. It also positions you to reinforce expectations of good performance.

Who do you need to follow up with this week?

NAME	COMPANY	TYPE OF FOLLOW UP	BY WHEN

Track Your Results

Most of you probably set goals each week, month or quarter on sales and revenue. You may also set goals on number of calls, appointments, proposals you make. You may track your cycle time from your first contact with them until they become a client. Those are all important goals to set and track.

What goals will you set for networking? What will you track? In step 0, you set goals for networking. Refine that list and document them below.

ACTIVITY	GOAL/FREQUENCY	ACTUAL

Here are some examples of goals you may want to track:

MONTHLY TRACKING	GOAL	ACTUAL
Number of networking events attended:	2	3
Number of referrals given:	1	1
Number of referrals received:	0	0
Number of thank you notes/articles sent:		
Number of follow ups done:		

Networking Map:

This tool can help you continue to refine who your most significant networking and referral sources are. The Networking Map looks like a mind map, where you begin with a referral source, and branch out to each person they referred to you. When you have a big cluster, you have a strong referral source. When you have many linkages, that person is a great connector, connecting you to many additional referral sources.

Write Your Mind Map Picture Here (see page 29 for reference.)

In addition, you may want to build a habit of regular networking activity. One tool you may find helpful is a Networking Points Tracking System.

List the key networking activities that are productive for your business first. For example:

~ Weekly leads group meeting
~ After work networking events
~ Sending thank you notes
~ Giving a referral
~ Asking a client for a referral

List yours here:

Now assign a point value to them that defines their effectiveness in helping you deliver results. Effectiveness is made up by a combination of value you receive ($$) and investment of time and/or energy. Point values should be from 1 – low level of effectiveness…3 medium level ….5 high level of effectiveness

	POINT VALUE
1. Weekly leads group meeting	3
2. After work networking events	3
3. Sending thank you notes	1
4. Giving a referral	4
5. Asking a client for a referral	5
6. Attending a strategic organization meeting	3
7. In a leadership role at a strategic meeting	5

Now set a goal for yourself. How many points will you target to get every week? For example, if you target to get 15 points each week, you can either ask 3 clients for a referral, or give a referral and send 5 thank you notes, and attend a leads group meeting and an after work networking event. Or you can send 15 thank you notes. Any combination that adds up to a 15 point counts. You decide the point values and you decide which activities to include.

Over time, you will learn which activities deliver the best return on your investment and you will build the habit of weekly networking.

ACTIVITY	WEEK 1	WEEK 2	WEEK 3	WEEK 4	MONTH
Leads Group Meeting	1	1	1	1	4
After work networking event			1		1
Thank you notes		3		8	11
Give a referral			1		1
Ask for a referral					
Attend a strategic organization meeting		2			2
Leadership role at strategic organization meeting					
Total	1	6	3	9	19

You can also see where you have holes in your networking plans and build in additional value added strategic activities.

Networking Activity and Results Tracking: Month / Year:

1. Track your activity:

Networking events attended: Goal: **3** Actual: **2**

NAME	COMPANY	MET?	ACKNOWLEDGED?	NEXT STEPS?	RESULT
Joe Smith	ABA Co.	GMA AWN	Thank you note	Call 2/13	Mtg.

2. Track the best referral sources for you: By network, organization and resource.

Referrals received: Goal: **4** Actual: **3**

NETWORK/ORG	# REFERRALS	F/U	VALUE $	INVESTMENT
BNI	2	2	150	30 hours
Chamber	1	1	250	3 hours

NETWORK/ORG	# REFERRALS	F/U	VALUE $	INVESTMENT
H. Jones	2	2	130	2 hours
B. Binny	1	1	225	2 days

3. Track your giving:

REFERRALS GIVEN	TO WHOM/CO.	DATE	RESULTS
Pass Printing	Ron Kennedy/IT Plus	4/03	Business
Organize U-Self	Steve Prest/Travel Now	4/03	No Business

OTHER GIVING	TO WHOM/CO.	DATE	PURPOSE/NEXT STEPS
Took to lunch	Jean Start/Secure Sys.	5/03	Info gathering/lunch 6/03

4. Ongoing follow up: Options: call, email, note, article, referral, included a colleague in your article, etc...

CONTACT	LAST FOLLOW UP	DATE	NEXT F/U DATE
Bill Kapen	call	3/15/03	5/12/03

5. Visibility:

	GOAL	ACTUAL	COST	IMPACT
Speaking	2	3	20	0
Articles published	1	1	2 hours	Sue Sar called
Ads	0	0	0	0

Be Accountable to the Program

You're in the home stretch. You know what you need to do to put together an implementation plan that will increase your networking capacity and ultimately increase your business results.

There are several considerations in this last step.

A. Build and use your plan. This step is the most important step of the process, because it is where all of your work comes together into your final implementation plan. If you've been building your plan all along, this final phase can be straightforward. If not, it will require reviewing all of the previous steps and pulling out the key information to form the plan.

B. Measure your results. Your implementation plan includes key measures. Tracking those key measures will give you the data you need to evaluate your progress.

C. Stay on track. Find an accountability buddy to work with to help you stay accountable to the plan. You have put a lot of energy and effort into your networking capacity and plan, make sure you plan in how to maintain it. Consider a member of your success team, a colleague, or a coach to help you stay on track.

D. Change your plan, when necessary. If you are not seeing the results you expect after about six months of full implementation, it may be time to change an aspect of your plan. Look at each piece of it and adjust what is not delivering for you.

Your implementation plan is an evolving, changing document. Treat it as a road map. Change it when it isn't working for you any more. The key component areas to include in your plan may never change, but the application may. In other words, you will always build a net of resources, but those specific resources that will best serve you may change. You will always need to talk about your business but your specific 60 second commercial may change.

Thank you for joining me on this networking journey. You have the tools you need now to become a master networker. The challenge is to take those tools into action. Bring all of what you have learned into your daily life, and enjoy the journey.

Abby Donnelly
Founder, networkingworks!

www.ingramcontent.com/pod-product-compliance
Lightning Source LLC
LaVergne TN
LVHW070146110826
845147LV00002B/334

* 9 7 8 0 9 8 2 5 0 7 8 0 3 *